Exp er

or

Adam Slowman, "Is your door open?" (Ps. 62:1, 5): being some fireside thoughts for the King's pensioners

With:

Conflicting Duties

And:

When the King Comes *to* His Own!

Emily Steele Elliott

Rough Draft Printing
1892

ISBN 978-1-60386-608-8

Contents

Expectation Corner

IT was New Year's Eve. Distant bells rang out mingled Christmas and New Year's messages to a joyous rhythm of their own; and, as from the great city came up in deep undertone a continuous roar of human life and occupation, I wondered as to the homes, rich and poor,—as to the hearts, outwardly severed though truly united,—in which those messages would meet with a responsive echo.

Then my eye fell on the Book before me; and the words on which it lighted seemed to sound out an answering Christmas chime, which had there taken form and shape, "Truly my soul waiteth upon God: from Him cometh my salvation!"

"For unto us a child is born!
For unto us a son is given!"

rang the bells.

"From Him Cometh My Salvation!" rang out again from the Psalm-book; "He only is my Rock and my Salvation!" "All my salvation and all my desire!" In the quietness of a solitary room, to which times and seasons bring little outer change, chimes of Heaven often linger and repeat themselves, as is only possible in the stilled atmosphere from which earth's louder voices are shut out.

And, as the twilight fell, it seemed to me that, all at once, the bells sounded forth other words through the frosty air—words as of bugle-call for the coming year:

"Now wait thou only upon God!
My expectation is from Him!"

and a bright flicker from the fire wakened up the same message from the old hereditary Psalm of royal melody, so that it stood out almost with the vividness of a new inscription:

"My Expectation Is From Him!"

Is it? And for what? And for how much? The thought would not be dismissed— rather, was bidden to remain.

How much am I expecting? How much do I know of waiting upon God? Should I be very much surprised if all my desires were visibly, actually to be fulfilled now?

Then came thoughts of humiliation— thoughts of contrition. So much promised! so little expected! So much chartered! so little claimed! So much praying? so little watching! No: so little praying! so little conscious receiving!

Ah! it all was too true; and on and on rang the notes in clear octave of harmony:

"My soul, wait only upon God:
My expectation is from Him!"

Then, after a while, my thoughts wandered to a seaside parish belonging to the history of other days, and to one home and another inhabited by those who had learned secrets of communication with Heaven, concerning which many of us seemed but poor scholars. And, as other memories intertwined themselves with these of sacred association, portraits from the past and present stood forth in the gloom with almost lifelike vividness, and, in half-allegory, shaped themselves into the history here, as for old cottage friends, set forth in homely words, which history may be called:

"A Chronicle *of the* Redeemed Land"

It ran thus:

Adam Slowman lived in a cottage on the Redeemed Land, which was a portion of an estate so large that—go which way you would—you could not see beyond it. The Owner of this land was honored far and near; and, on the particular part of the property to which Adam belonged, He was most especially loved and obeyed. The reason why it was called the Redeemed Land, was that, after a rebellion a long time before, which had brought the people to what looked like hopeless ruin, His own Son had, by actually coming and living like a poor cottager amongst them, and toiling as one of them, worked out a plan for their being taken once more into favor, by paying in His own person the fine which had been laid on them as a forfeit for their evil doings.

So, ever after, all whose names were down in the petition which was sent up to the Lord of the estate asking forgiveness for the past, and claiming right to a part in the payment worked out by His Son, who had made Himself their Brother in sorrow and trouble, received special promises of love and favor. To each one a lease or covenant was given, by which he held his house and ground—a lease promising him many and various rights and grants for himself and his family—with the assurance that, although at some time, sooner or later, he might have to give them up, he should have a far better and more lasting home in a glorious province of his Lord's kingdom—nay, in the glories of His own out-stretching palace—when home and hearth should fail here.

If I were to tell you half the good things of this Redeemed Land, you would be surprised at the love and kindness with which it was cared for by the Owner. Though around it much of the estate lay waste, every house there had its claim to a supply of the purest water, specially, and with boundless care, brought over the hills for its inhabitants. Then there were fair meadows and quiet woods, to which each one had a pass-key and right of admission; and there were orchards with rich fruit to be had for the asking, and all manner of other privileges by the covenant of each house placed within reach of the humblest cottager, which mention of tenant rights brings me back to my story of Adam Slowman.

He was getting on in life, was Adam, and he had for a long time been settled in his house on the Redeemed Land, which, if you look carefully in the map of the property, is written down there as the "*Land of Forgiveness of Sin.*" But he was a slow scholar, and used to grumble that his sight wasn't so good as it might be in looking up his covenant, which all the same he held to firm and fast, as his one security for the promises on which he counted.

Adam lived poor, so to speak, when he might have lived rich. His windows were dull and clouded, when, if only he had rubbed away the cobwebs and dust which darkened them, a glad sunshine would always have brightened every room in the cottage. He complained of a want of fresh water; but, as his next-door neighbor often reminded him, he had only to see that his own pipe, connecting his place with the living fountain from the hills, was kept clear and open, to have enough and over without stint or hindrance.

Then he used sometimes to bemoan himself that food was scarce. "Why, man," said his next-door neighbor, Widow Full- joy, when she heard this, "you're bringing up words, in saying that, which seem like accusing our Lord and Master of keeping His tenants half-starved! Isn't His own granary, where food enough is stored for generations to come, right there in sight of our windows, and all you need bought and paid for, that you might have it free? You must know as well as I do that you've only to give in a petition, and get it rightly signed, and wait for the answer, to have, day by day, enough, not only to keep you from starving, but, what's more, to make your countenance appear fatter and fresher than that of the children of any other king!"

"Ah, neighbor," Adam would reply, in a voice as dreary as the wind in winter, "you're right, I often do believe! But you seem to get hold of things which I can't. That oil of joy for mourning, found to you year by year, is what I don't see how I'm ever to come in for. I don't think it's down in my covenant; no, nor clothes like yours. That garment of praise for the spirit of heaviness, which our visitor said the other day was the livery we are all expected to wear down this way—it's a deal richer clothing than, it seems to me, I've got a right to put on, poor and worthless as I am. I do thank Him in my poor way for all He's done for me, but—but—"

"But do you think it's humbler to tune '*O come let us sing unto the Lord; let us heartily rejoice in the strength of our salvation!*' to the Dead March in the Lamentations," put in Widow Fulljoy, with energy, "or to sound it out, or, what's nearer the truth, sorrow it out, as if it was somebody else's praising you'd got to do by mistake, having no right to a thanksgiving of your own? Why, man, people had best put on black crape over their helmets of salvation to show their humility in that sort of praising, instead of looking right up to the One who's saved them with, 'He loved me and gave Himself for me,' in their song."

"Now, I *do* think you're a bit too strong there, neighbor," said poor Adam meekly; "if you were as poor as I am, you'd know how hard it is to sound out one's thanks like that. I wouldn't be the one to bring a discredit on my dear Lord, no not for all the world; but, you see, we're different. We're the same family, I know, but—but— you're a richer branch. Yes—there it is!" repeated Adam, as if he had got hold of a new light with a ray of comfort in it: "I feel as if I was a sort of poor relation to you, and couldn't ever hope for all that's granted to those with stronger faith."

"'Poor relation,' man! and pray what call have you to be poor, with bank-notes there hidden away between the leaves of your Covenant-book, which are never so much as taken out and presented? I do declare," she said, half to herself, "he's like that poor crazy nobleman down in the shires that was richer than a prince, and had got the notion into his head that he was nigh on bankrupt, and half starved himself and his family as well, and died after years of leading the life of a pauper.

"Dear old friend," she continued gently, "*do* think that it's hard on a rich Father— loving as He's rich—when His children go poorly clad and complaining of scarcity. But I see how it is: you're weak and you're getting on in years, and you feel as if it was too much for your head to be thinking out a deal of what's told us in our covenant of our Lord's plans of providing for His own. So it seems to me what you've got to do is to ask Him to do the remembering for you as well as the giving; that's it," she nodded to herself—"the remembering and the giving both—the seeing what you want and the making it good out of His great love and riches. I know for certain, neighbor, if only you send in a petition like that to his great house, He'll see to it directly and answer it."

"But how shall I put it into words, neighbor?" said Adam. "Somehow my petitions only seem to get to Him now and then; you're a deal a better scholar than I, now that I'm old and a bit dim of sight and slow of understanding."

"Well, it seems to me there are words ready found for us," answered Widow Fulljoy, going to a cupboard in which Adam's Covenant-book was carefully kept. Here are some:

"'Lord, I am oppressed; undertake for me!
Plead Thou the causes of my soul!
Arise, O Lord, plead Thine own cause!
Be surety unto Thy servant for good.'

"'Show me Thy ways, O Lord: teach me Thy paths. Lead me in Thy truth, and teach me: for Thou art the God of my salvation: on Thee do I wait all the day. Remember, O Lord, Thy tender mercies and Thy loving kindnesses: for they have been ever of old. Remember not the sins of my youth, nor my transgressions: according to Thy mercy, remember Thou me, for Thy goodness' sake, O Lord!'

"Send in those words, Adam, and see what they will bring you. Here you must add: 'This petition comes from My Lord's humble servant, who is waiting with open door for his Lord's answer'"

"If only He will deign to read it and send an answer!" sighed Adam doubtfully.

"If only!" echoed Widow Fulljoy, with a sort of receipt in advance in her tone. "Why, neighbor, one would think you lived in the land of condemnation instead of the Land of Forgiveness of Sin! 'a land of hills and valleys, and which drinketh water of the rain of heaven: a land which our Lord careth for: the eyes of our Lord always upon it, from the beginning of the year even unto the end of the year.' *If only*! I know how it was with me when I sent in that very same petition, long ago, and how, with all sorts of blessed incomings, I got back this note with the postmark from my Lord's own palace—'Good and upright is the Lord: therefore will He teach sinners in the way. The meek will He guide in judgment; and the meek will He teach His way. All the paths of the Lord are mercy and truth unto such as keep His covenant and His testimonies.' Oh, it was brave to get a token like that," she added, "and all as true as the sunlight."

"At all events I shall hope something may come of it," answered Adam. "I don't want to seem ungrateful, neighbor," he still murmured, "but often and often when I *have* sent a petition, and really from my heart, it hasn't seemed to make much difference."

"I wonder whether you've seen to the terms of our Covenant-book," was the reply. "The sending in the petition isn't all. There are three parts to that blessed trade with the palace of our Lord. Look here, it says, 'CONTINUE *in prayer*,' then 'WATCH in the same'; and then, when you've watched—and when did he ever tell you to watch in vain?—*then*" continued Widow Fulljoy triumphantly, "then the *thanksgiving*. Ah! that *thanksgiving*! it's like all one's life-joy worked up into a psalm."

It was with a half-sigh of relief that Adam signed his name to his petition. After he had written it down, and put it into the post-office set up beside his door by the Lord of the estate, he seemed ever so much lighter while his old friend showed him in his own book a record of how that same Lord had cared for His people long ago, when they were cast down and too low to take hold of the promises which were there waiting for them to claim.

"It's written out here," she said, "where it's told how they were monished and brought low."

"Like me!" put in Adam.

"And they couldn't bring to mind all that He was ready to give them—too dull, so to speak, to read, and too short of memory to remember, and too low down almost to hope. And see here what it says, man: 'He remembered FOR THEM this covenant!' Ah, that's what I was saying! He did the remembering as well as the giving. He pleaded with Himself, so to speak, for what He knew was promised in His own mind for them; and He gave it them, not because they were clever in asking, but because He read in his own word loads and loads of meaning which they couldn't understand, but which for His own sake He wanted to make good to them.

"Why, there's rights and privileges in our covenants, Adam, which are as much greater than anything we can understand as are the very accounts of Heaven itself. It came to me long ago how my Lord would be honored in my getting hold of more of His riches, and living out more like a king's daughter, and having her place according, and a song of His goodness always telling of a full store. And I thought how much more there was in His promises than I could even call to mind; and so, as I put Him in remembrance of one and another, I said, in my petition, 'But oh, my Lord, there's more in that than I can think or tell, but Thou knowest Thine own mind to give, and Thine own riches in glory; so do Thou remember for me Thy covenant, and send the answer accordingly, and Thy servant's door will be open for Thy gifts, and my heart expecting and my eyes waiting for Thy coming!' And I got such a store, and am always getting more, that I've learned to see He means what He says. And so do you the same, Adam; and then—what's more—thank Him!"

And as Widow Fulljoy went out into the sunshine, and turned into her own little house, where a wealth of peace and treasures of hope and comfort all round told of a bounteous Giver, Adam heard her favorite song, ringing out through the stillness:

"When long ago I took Thee at Thy word,
My sins were washed away;
Now for all else I claim Thy promise, Lord,
As mine for every day!

"Be mine the stream from everlasting hills—
Thy Spirit's boundless grace;
Be mine the peace which lowliest temple fills
Where Thou hast dwelling-place.

"Be mine with rich provision to show forth
    The bounty of my King!
Full stores of grace should tell His boundless worth
    Whose royal love I sing.

"Oh! for receiving that shall glorify
    The Lord whom I implore!
My listening soul entreats Him to draw nigh,
    And waits with open door."

* * * * * * *

The Messenger visits Adam

Adam had not long to wait after sending in his petition to the Great House. Through his open door a Messenger came all silently to his side, with words of blessing and peace.

"You called for me in your petition, and wrote, 'Show me Thy ways and teach me Thy paths!' so I have come, Adam," he said; "but your house is dark, and your place is scantily furnished, and you seem starved and poorly clothed, instead of living like the King's own."

Adam looked sad and ashamed. "It's all true, my Lord," he said. "I seem too low down to help myself, and too unworthy to get hold of better things, though I love my Kingly Master and do praise Him for putting me in this Redeemed Land, and for so frankly forgiving all my debt, and letting me look up to Him as my Friend and Sovereign Ruler."

The Visitor looked pityingly and yet sadly upon him, and then went to the window and breathed upon it. And in a little the sunlight streamed in right upon Adam, and lit up the page where his Covenant- book lay open, and fell upon the words, "ALL THINGS ARE YOURS," so that they stood out in new fresh light to his eyes, while, from Widow Fulljoy's cottage, a scrap of a hymn, which she was singing as she stood at her door, was borne on the wind. The words sounded out:

"Thy blessed unction from above
    Is comfort, life, and fire of love;
Enable with perpetual light
    The dullness of our blinded sight!"

Then the Visitor looked to where a scanty supply of clouded water told part of the reason of Adam's being weak and low; and, going to where the connection lay for a supply from the hill fountains, he cleared out so much rubbish from the pipe that you would have wondered how anyone could have got enough to live on, let alone thriving. Then, when the clear stream, with life and healing in every drop, began to flow in, and Adam's Visitor brought him a full draught, you wouldn't have known him for the same man! There came such a light to his eyes, and such a firmness to his limbs, which had been trembling like one in the palsy, that already you could see that he was being nourished from the King's country.

Then the Visitor looked at the cupboard and found a few bits of bread which had lain there some time, good and pure bread, indeed, but so scanty, and left so long, that the question came once more as to how Adam had been getting on at all.

"Stale manna isn't our Lord's plan for His tenants," he said; "new corn of the land is what He has for his people—the bread from His own palace. It seems to me, Adam, that it is long since you had yours fresh. Why, even in the rebellious provinces it's told abroad how 'the Lord hath visited his people in giving them bread.'"

"It's all true, my Lord," was the answer, and Adam looked with something of shame at his shelves; "but—but—I fall back upon what I keep there, and am thankful not to be quite starved."

"Quite starved, man!" was the reply, "quite starved! and you living on the Redeemed Land, and the store wagons coming past your door each day with 'MERCIES NEW EVERY MORNING' written up in large letters on them, and the parcels ready to give in for each one who has the receipt ready—'GREAT IS THY FAITHFULNESS.' *Starved*! When the fruits are there from the Lord's own gardens—provisions from His own house! Starved! When there's such planning, and care, and forethought put into making up every supply for each one of His tenants every day, that to undo it and take out these new mercies that are sent, and hold them up to the light, and see them unfolding, and mark them fitting into every need that comes through all the hours, makes the whole day like a gift-day, which it is, and its song, 'Whoso is wise and will observe these things, even he shall understand the loving kindness of the Lord!'

"But what's been the matter, Adam, has been that your door has been shut, or only half open now and then. The stores have been there for you, but there's been no one looking out to take them in day by day. Every now and then, indeed, just a little chink has been unfastened—enough for a bit of bread here and a stray fruit there, but little more than starvation allowance; and you bringing discredit on your royal Lord by little expecting and little receiving.

"Then your petitions, Adam, have had so many 'ifs' and 'buts'—there have come along with them so many 'I don't expects' and 'perhapses,' and so many 'I don't know whether this'll ever get into my Lord's hands, and if it does, I don't know whether He'll hear me,' that they've been—though you mayn't have meant them so—half insults to His goodness. As if He had paid such a price for setting up His royal posts that there should be a doubt as to His receiving and seeing to any petition sent out to Him in due course, and according to His orders, and made in His Son's name!"

"I never meant—I don't think I ever put such words into my petitions," faltered Adam; "I know they were often badly written, for I'm a poor scholar—but—but—"

"Scholar, man! There are thousands and thousands of letters which go straight into His Dead Letter Office which are all made up of dictionary words, and of what people outside call fine scholarship. No! 'Remember Thy word unto Thy servant upon which Thou hast caused me to hope!' has the scholarship in it which brings in the answer. 'God be merciful to me a sinner!' which, for His Son's sake, long ago procured for you the free pardon and the place on this property—everyone in the House giving way before that petition—had no fine words sent in with it. Humility and confession of sin are the first lessons which are taught in your Lord's own school, set up for those whom He would have on His estate; and humility and trust on-and-on are the next. Look to your Covenant-book, Adam, for it seems to me you've stopped low down in the classes, and see what scholarship is needed for the petitions that get in and are heard by Him. '*This poor man cried, and the Lord heard him and delivered him out of all his troubles.*' '*For the oppression of the poor, for the sighing of the needy, now will I arise, saith the Lord*!" There's the scholarship—the cry and the sighs—then the watching and the praise.

"Why, you know, Adam, that your Lord's own Son, who paid such a price to free you, and get you a place on the estate, makes it His business to sign every petition sent in in His name. And look how He is longing to give each one what is best and needful for him! He left these words for all who should seek pardon through Him, the very last night of His being down here, to work out by His own suffering a right to His Father's love and gifts of blessing; 'Verily, verily, I say unto you, Whatsoever ye shall ask the Father in My Name, He will give it you. Hitherto have ye asked nothing in My Name: ask, and ye shall receive, that your joy may be full.' That's what you may call a fine bank-note for one on the royal estate; but remember that, when you're sending in a petition, every '*if*' and '*but*,' and '*It's pretty much a chance if I'm heard*!' and '*I don't feel as if my prayer would get much higher than the ceiling*!" and '*I don't think*

I'm likely to have an answer!' comes out as a great blot, and sometimes covers up the writing, so that it scarcely gets read.

"There are no ifs and buts about those words in your Covenant-book: 'The Lord upholdeth all that fall, and raiseth up all those that be bowed down. The eyes of all wait upon Thee: and Thou givest them their meat in due season. Thou openest Thine hand, and satisfiest the desire of every living thing. The Lord is righteous in all His ways, and holy in all His works. The Lord is nigh unto all them that call upon Him, to all that call upon Him in truth. He will fulfill the desire of them that fear Him: He also will hear their cry, and will save them.' That's the way the supplies come in for those who see to it that there's nothing between them and their receiving from the royal storehouse. *'My soul, wait thou only upon God, for my expectation is from Him!'* There, Adam, put down in plain figures how much you've expected from Him, and you'll see why you've gone on in this shabby half-alive fashion! Now come with me!"

Adam travels with his Guide

And very swiftly Adam found himself carried away to a part of the estate of which he had, indeed, heard, but which he had never expected to see. A long range of storehouses met his eye, from which heavily laden wagons were going forth to all parts of the property, bringing out supplies, sometimes exactly according to the petitions sent in from the tenants themselves, which were kept in a book for reference, and often in stores and gifts which the Lord of the property, who knew everything about each one, saw to be better suited for them than the very things they asked for. Over these storehouses was written in large letters:

"The Lord over all is rich unto all that call upon Him."

And underneath:

"The expectation of the poor shall not perish."

But from these Adam's Guide turned away to a huge outbuilding some distance off in the shade, and said, "Do you know what this is, Adam?"

"No, my Lord," was the answer.

"This," said the Messenger, "is the 'MISSED BLESSINGS OFFICE.' Here are kept stores and gifts which were all ready to be sent forth for many, who, for one cause or another, never received them, one common reason being that the door was closed when the store-chariots came round. That door of expectation—though you would hardly believe it—many keep shut, even when they have sent in a request for the very thing which is supplied for their need, and though they write in their petition, '*On Thee do I wait all the day.*'"

Adam looked shy and uneasy at these words, and still more so when his Guide opened the gate of the outer court, and led him through the large halls. Such numbers of parcels, all with the date of their sending out, and, alas! each one telling of its having missed an owner.

Over one department of these stores, where quantities of raw material lay massed, was written up, "YE HAVE NOT, BECAUSE YE ASK NOT."

Over a second, "Your sins have withholden good things from you."

Over a third, "THEY LIMITED THE HOLY ONE OF ISRAEL." "LET NOT THAT MAN THAT DOUBTETH THINK THAT HE SHALL RECEIVE ANYTHING OF THE LORD! "and just underneath was a handbill, with the words, "*Doors found closed, and no entrance for chartered gifts.*"

Over another was the inscription, "CONDITIONS UNFULFILLED"; and a placard underneath bore the notice:

> "If ye abide in Me, and My words abide in you,
> ye shall ask what ye will,
> and it shall be done unto you.
> Bring ye all the tithes into the storehouse,
> that there may be meat in Mine house,
> and PROVE ME NOW herewith,
> saith the Lord of hosts,
> if I will not open you the windows of heaven,
> and pour you out a blessing,
> that there shall not be room enough to receive it."

Over one darkly and distantly seen store was written: "FORFEITED BLESSINGS"; and underneath, "*Ye ask, and receive not, because ye ask amiss, that ye may consume it upon your lusts.*"

Meanwhile Adam's face grew more and more downcast, as he saw the riches, the royal provisions, the packages prepared with bounteous care, which would have made thousands rich and happy, lying neglected. But he had yet more to learn. His Guide led him quickly into the third of the chambers, which opened out into the large court, and there, ranged in order, were what seemed endless parcels, all sorted on shelves with the names written above them of those for whom they had been sent out, and who had yet never received them.

Before one range of shelves the Messenger stopped. The name written up over these was "*Adam Slowman.*" Adam gazed in mute surprise. Those crowded shelves! The very things stored closely together for which he had wished, and had now and then asked, with many a blot, however, on his petition; treasures which, though they were there for him, he had not received.

"I thought the line was blocked often and often," he said, as he glanced at the labels outside the parcels, and read, "Strength for work," "Support in sickness," "Extra comforts for the winter," "Seed for sowing," "Opportunities for service," "Stores for Christmas-keeping," "New Years gifts," with the words written underneath this parcel: "If ye, being evil, know how to give good gifts unto your children how much more shall your Father which is in heaven give good things to them that ask Him!"

How Adam longed to open that box! Then he saw that it was dated three years before, when he had been so low down—so ill and poor—that he had gone on saying over and over, "Thou hast covered Thyself with a cloud, that my prayer should not pass through."

"The block was at your own door, Adam, you see," was the grave observation. "That box is of the kind which your Lord uses for His choicest gifts."

"And! why! I *do* declare!" exclaimed Adam, in amaze, "if a shining silvery garment isn't there, hanging up, such as I told Widow Fulljoy might be for her, but couldn't be for one low and poor like me!" And high up above his head sparkled, indeed, a glistening robe made exactly to his size, and bearing the label, "THE GARMENT OF PRAISE."

"And *there's* something else! "he said with a sorrowful surprise, "all ready labeled for me in that crystal bottle! How little I knew! 'OIL OF JOY FOR MOURNING!' And more and more! What's that up there? If my eyes don't deceive me, that's the very thing I went moaning and groaning for the want of, till I pretty near wore out everyone's patience!" and he pointed to a basket of fairest make, which had once been wreathed round with hearts' ease and moss, so tenderly that you saw love and planning in every bit, though the flowers had faded and the moss withered. On it were the words, "ABUNDANCE OF PEACE."

"That's our Lord's own handwriting," said the Messenger gravely. "You see it was dated in the drought season years ago."

"My sore time of need!" said Adam; "and I wrote down that day in my private book, '*For peace I had bitterness*,' because I thought my Lord was displeased and hiding His favors from me; and that he hadn't read my petition."

"But you kept your door shut, Adam; you never went to your Covenant-book and saw that the peace was in your birthright, or remembered that the petition was taken from your Lord's own promise, and that, if He was true, what you had to do was to look out for it as sure as the sun shines, because His Son brought it for you Himself."

"And that lamp, up in the corner, and those glasses: they've got my name on them too!" continued Adam, exploring farther and farther, with a sort of sadness in his voice.

His Guide took them down. "I gave out those glasses for you," he said. "Here is a bit of your own writing tacked to the parcel!" and he read the words, "*Open Thou mine eyes that I may behold wondrous things out of Thy law!*"

"Ah! that's what I always put up before I look to my Covenant-book," said Adam; "and I've sometimes longed to understand more, but have seemed to see so little. My neighbor, now, she's always boasting of her glasses, and sees to read so much that my poor eyes never could make out that it's like a surprise to me all she finds out in her book."

"Did you ever *expect* to get them, or look out for fresh light to be sent to you on your Lord's own word?" asked his Guide. "Why, man, there are promises and promises in that Covenant-book and bank-notes let in to the pages, and revealings of all that your Lord wants to do for you in befriending you, that you never see without His extra light, which I myself prepared for you in this very lamp, and without this second-sight, so to speak, which you, as well as your neighbor, might have had with these glasses, which are called ' Opening of eyes to the blind.'

"But now it is time to come away. Only remember, Adam, that our Lord is so good and gracious that I am not without a hope that some of these treasures may yet find their way to your cottage, and when He passes by and looks at it, it may have ceased to bring such a discredit on His love as it does now."

But, as they passed, a large detached building caught Adam's glance which he had not noticed before.

"May I know the meaning of that fine storehouse?" he asked. "The royal crown is above the entrance, so it must, I gather, be of our Lord's building up."

His Guide turned toward it. "It is a Royal Exchange Office, Adam," he replied. "Many a petition cannot be answered just as poor short-sighted people think best. To get according to their prayers would often be their misery. That place is where our Lord Himself considers these applications and changes His grants to what is really most for their good. Some pray for life here, and they get life forever and ever beyond. Some ask for success and speedy deliverance, and they get disappointments which bring them nearer to Him who will deliver them gloriously in trouble, if not always out of trouble. Some ask for health of body, and they get health of soul instead, and learn what it is to gain the highest attainable gift of a submitted will, which brings changeless peace, and is worth all the prosperity gifts put together. Oh, if only people knew all the care that our Lord gives to the exchanges carried on for His own in what is called the '*Commuted Petitions Department*,' they would wonder at His love in caring to do all this for their good with never a failure!"

"And may I yet once more be allowed to ask the name of that more distant store, which has a large and peculiar sort of clock over it, and a sun-dial in front?" said Adam, pointing to a well-sheltered building toward which some empty wagons were being rapidly driven. "Over the gates the inscription looks to me like 'THOUGH IT TARRY, WAIT!'"

"That," said the Guide, "is the 'DELAYED BLESSINGS STORE OFFICE.' Take this glass, and you will read underneath the words:

"'Therefore will the Lord wait,
    that He may be gracious unto you:
And therefore will He be exalted,
    that He may have mercy upon you:
For the Lord is a God of judgment:
    Blessed are all they that wait for Him.'

"That clock never goes too fast or too slow, and is so constructed that, when the shadow on the dial shows that 'the time of the promise draws nigh,' it sounds, as an alarm, a warning to the messengers to be ready at once for the delivery of the stored blessings, which, the moment that 'the fullness of the time is come,' are sent forth from the gates. It's not always that the petitioners' doors are found open; for delayed blessings too often come as a surprise even to the Lord's constant remembrancers. When they are still found waiting, and expecting after long tarrying, they receive a '*Great is thy faith! be it unto thee even as thou wilt*!' which they are not likely to forget.

"It takes a long time for some pensioners to learn that 'Delays are not denials.' Zacharias would not believe even the angel-messenger who told him the blessing was on its way to his house; and not for many a month was his tongue, tied because of unbelief, loosed to send in the thanksgiving. When the blessings came to the door of Mary of Jerusalem, in the shape of Peter himself, after only a little season of waiting, the very people who had been day and night getting up and sending out petitions for his deliverance would not believe that their Lord had heard them; and while the answer was knocking at the closed gate outside, they cried to the portress who told its coming, 'Thou art mad!'

The Romans had been petitioning for three years that Paul might come to them; but there were good reasons why the blessing was delayed. A tumult, a hurricane, and a shipwreck were all put in harness to bring him to their doors, bound as a prisoner; but yet their petition that he might have 'a prosperous journey by the will of God, in order that he might impart unto them some spiritual gift,' was made good as neither he nor they had expected: and in far richer measure for the delay. Onesimus and Philemon were among those who found that out.

"Ah, there are secrets of love and wisdom in the workings of the 'Delayed Blessings Department' which are little dreamed of!" added the Guide gravely. "Men would pluck their mercies green, when their Lord would have them ripe; but if only they knew the preciousness in His sight of the faith that can wait and trust in the dark, they would understand more of His words: '*Strengthened according to His glorious power unto all patience. Wait, I say, on the Lord*!'"

The Wagon prepared for "Expectation Corner"

Then they went back into the sunshine, and, leaving behind them the various buildings connected with the "Missed Blessings Offices," passed once again by the royal storehouses which they had seen at the first. A wagon was being laden in the front court by the servants, who were making ready to start. It seemed to Adam, from the anxious care bestowed, that some very choice packages were being lifted into it, and, to his surprise, the name of his old neighbor was written in full upon one or two which at once met his eyes.

"Is this your afternoon delivery?" asked his Guide.

"It's morning and afternoon and evening to that pensioner," was the answer. "*Expectation Corner* we call her place. And our Lord Himself sees so much to each package going out to her door, that you'd think He had hardly anyone else to care for. Her petitions! why they come up so fast, that if there were any end to these stores, and if there were many more like her, we'd be going bankrupt! But '*Ask, and ye shall receive*,' is the word here; and '*riches in glory*' don't lessen by giving, and His orders are '*Men ought always to pray and not to faint*,' It's seldom we pass Widow Fulljoy's door that she isn't waiting for us with a smile and a receipt ready, and with arms stretched out for her gifts, and with '*Bless the Lord, O my soul, and forget not all His benefits*!' for her psalm of thanks. A good bit of our work down in that part of the estate will be over soon, I guess, when the widow's place is empty, and her petitions stop coming in."

"So her call is near at hand?" said Adam's Guide, as he glanced at the parcels directed to her.

"Aye, they do say that our Lord has pretty nigh finished getting ready the rooms in His own palace where she is to live royally with Him, and that all her petitions which she has been sending in these years and years will show out in a deal of the bravery that's been making ready for her. She'll not be wanting much more of their ministry, I reckon, who are sent down to minister to the heirs of the Salvation Land!"

Adam glanced at the labels on one or two of the packages which bore Widow Fulljoy's name. On the first—which seemed like a crystal cup containing some precious cordial—was written, "STRENGTH FOR ENDURANCE," and the words were underneath, "*In the day when thou calledst I answered thee, and strengthened thee with strength in thy soul*." As was often the custom in the sending out of the parcels from the royal storehouses, the petition, in her own handwriting, which had claimed the gift, was attached to it as a memorandum, and Adam recognized it in a moment, as he read the words: "*I will go in the strength of the Lord God: I will make mention of Thy righteousness, even of Thine only. O God, Thou hast taught me from my youth: and hitherto have I declared Thy wondrous works. Now also when I am old and gray-headed, O God, forsake me not: until I have showed Thy strength unto this generation, and Thy power to everyone that is to come.*"

The next parcel was labeled "VIEWS OF THE HEAVENLY CITY AND ITS DELIGHTS."

And underneath the label you could read: "Eye hath not seen, nor ear heard, neither have entered into the heart of man, the things which God hath prepared for them that love Him, But God hath revealed them unto us by His Spirit."

"Ah!" said the Guide, "she will have a rare time with those views—'the evidences of things not seen.' See, there is an autograph note fastened to the clasp, '*Blessed is she that believed: for there shall be a performance of those things which were told her from the Lord.*'"

Another gift drew Adam's notice from its peculiar shape, and from the words of the address; for under the widow's name was written, "Poor of this world; rich in faith; and heir of the kingdom." Its form was like that of an Æolian harp; and even as he looked, a breath from his Guide on the strings brought forth sounds of such exquisite harmony that they seemed to Adam too ravishing for mortal ear. He fancied that the chords formed themselves into words which sounded like the echo from a distance of a chorus of voices singing, "*Worthy is the Lamb that was slain to receive power, and riches, and wisdom, and strength, and honor, and glory, and blessing.*"

"She is favored," said his Guide; "'the musical instruments of God' are still, as long ago, given out to the chosen among His praising ones. The music and the hymns of the royal palace will be echoed around her to the end, until the messenger choirs come down with the royal chariots to her own door, and chant the bridal song for the Homeward procession: '*Lo, the winter is past, the rain is over and gone: the flowers appear on the earth; the time of the singing of birds is come. My beloved spake, and said unto me, Rise up, my love, my fair one, and come away!*'"

Adam quite distinctly read a line or two of the supplication attached to the parcel in accordance with which this gift was sent.

"*As the hart panteth after the water brooks, so panteth my soul after Thee, O God. The Lord will command His loving kindness in the daytime, and in the night His song shall be with me.*"

But he might not stay longer. His Guide brought him swiftly back to the cottage which he had quitted to learn so much. There it was! poor and sad-looking enough; but the sunlight streamed in at the window as it had not done for many a day. And on the table where he had left it lay Adam's Covenant-book. The wind from the open casement played among its leaves, and, as he and his Guide came back into the room, the words, bathed in sunshine, glittered into sight, "*He that spared not His own Son, but delivered Him up for us all, how shall He not with Him also freely give us all things? It is Christ that died, yea rather that is risen again, who is even at the right hand of God, who also maketh intercession for us. Who shall separate us from the love of Christ?*"

Then "*The Lord fulfill all thy petitions*!" sounded like a strain of music through the room; and, when Adam turned round, his Visitor was gone.

Epilogue

I wish you could see Adam Slowman as he now is. You would think that Widow Fulljoy, when the royal carriages came down to take her to the palace, which they did before long, had left him a legacy of songs and praising. You would hear from his open door her favorite words ringing out:

"When long ago I took Thee at Thy word My sins were washed away; Now for all else I claim Thy promise, Lord, As mine for every day!"

If you could look into his cottage, you would see tokens of his Lord's love and thought on every shelf and in every corner, and you would hear of the mercy which had forgiven past doubts and misgivings concerning his royal Master's care, while he would tell you of how blessings which he had long missed had been graciously granted to him. He would go on joyfully to say how, day by day, he looks out for the King's messengers and welcomes the King's store-wagons. He would tell you of the green pastures and still waters outside, to which he has entrance in right of his tenancy on the Redeemed Land, and of his precious pass-key with "*The Lord is my Shepherd*" graven on the handle—the key which before he had allowed to get so rusty that it would scarcely turn in the locks of the gates admitting to different portions of the royal estates. He would tell you of the rich fruits which grow for him in the enclosed gardens, and of the sacred meetings with his Lord's own messenger, nay, with his Lord Himself; and of how, all through, that same gracious Sovereign has heard his petition, and has remembered for him the covenant and has made it good to him when he has been too weak, and often too short-sighted, to know all its meaning for himself. All this he would tell you, and much more. But I must pause.

The thought which has gone into this little story is so clear that its outworking can hardly be called that of an allegory. "*I perish with hunger*!" is, alas! the cry not always confined to the prodigal son. Are there not many of the Lord's own children who, placing their record of reception beside His charters of promise, are constrained to ask themselves whether indeed those promises in their fullness and freshness are still in force; whether the promissory notes on the King's storehouses are still honored for the procuring of all that they are set forth as bringing down from His hand?

Dear friend, what of our "ships of desire sent out to the land of spices and pearls"? What of our traffic with Heaven? "*My expectation is from Him!*" Is this really our motto, as it is the merchant's awaiting the return of treasure-laden vessels, sent forth empty to the unseen coast? Is our watchword "*On Thee do I wait all the day*"?

See how really St. Paul sent out definite petitions, and looked for and received the supplies: "Having therefore obtained help of God, I continue unto this day." "I know that this shall turn to my salvation through your prayers, and the supply of the Spirit of Jesus Christy according to my earnest expectation, and my hope that in nothing I shall be ashamed." There is no doubt here as to the line of communication being open between earth and Heaven.

It may be that this little book has fallen into the hands of one of the Royal Family of God—of one of His own children, living in the land of Forgiveness of Sin, and yet leading a life of spirit-poverty—of soul-penury. Dear friend, are you poor when you want to be rich? Are you mourning over empty vessels, while your Lord longs to pour you out a blessing that there shall not be room enough to receive it? If so, will you think over what is written for you in your own "Covenantbook"— God's Holy Word of Promise? Remember that no heart petition sent up in the name of Jesus Christ, our Sin-bearer and Intercessor, can lose its way between earth and Heaven. Remember that He is more ready to hear than we to pray. Remember that He still says, "According to your faith be it unto you," and that if you ask for the faith, He loves and longs to give it.

Shall not we, then, now, take up our stand at "EXPECTATION CORNER" more truly than ever before? Shall not we ask Him to enable us that we may live as should live the children of the King, showing forth His praise who hath made us, unto our God, kings and priests?

We may be low down, aged, weak in body, slow of speech, stricken with sorrow; but let us remember what stands written for us by one so far down, that from the depths of the sea, he cried, "The depths closed me round about: the weeds were wrapped about my head." Found he not that even from the ocean bed there was a path to Heaven, and to the ear of his Father?

"*When my soul fainted within me, I remembered the Lord, and my prayers came in unto Thee into Thine Holy Temple.*" And found he not also, to his joy, that there was, in like manner, a path for the Lord's mercy and help from the heights of heaven to the caverns of the sea? And when the deliverance came he forgot not the praise: "But I will sacrifice unto Thee with the voice of thanksgiving; I will pay that that I have vowed. Salvation *is* of the Lord."

So for us let the clear psalm note ring out to-day:

"MY SOUL, WAIT ONLY UPON GOD: MY EXPECTATION IS FROM HIM!"

And may the secret of Heaven, confided to the disciples when their Lord was about to leave them in a cold and dark world, be proved as of ever-fresh assurance by His chosen ones, to whom it has been handed down from generation to generation: "*Ask, and ye shall receive, that your joy may be full!*"

Conflicting Duties

Chapter I

"AND you see, my dear sir, I have so many contending claims! Home calls and charity calls, the family and the district. You, who must know far better than I what it is to be in the midst of conflicting duties, will understand my difficulty in this matter."

The speaker was a middle-aged and kindly-featured lady—hurried in manner and voice, but conveying in her whole person and speech an impression of benevolent and capable, though possibly of diffuse, activity. Her visit to Dr. Elwin's study on behalf of more than one family in her district was at an end; and this was the conclusion with which, gathering together sundry letters and papers, she prepared to say good-by.

A kindly smile was on the face of the venerable pastor, who knew well how to value Mrs. Stanton's generous and truehearted co-operation in parish interests; a smile, however, which worked itself into something like a visible note of inter-rogation as her farewell observation fell on his ear.

"Many *claims*, certainly; but I cannot, say that the experience of conflicting duties is one which I am prepared to recognize. If you will pardon me for seeming for a moment to differ from you I should be inclined to dispose of the expression as a contradiction in terms."

No conflicting duties! If only Dr. Elwin knew! If only he could see at that moment on her writing-desk at home the printed notice of the Zenana working-party, the list of clothes needed for the children's summer wardrobes, the house-books waiting to be made up, the half-finished letter to Herbert at college, the jotted- down notes for her mothers'-meeting address on the following Monday, the statement of cases for admission to the Servants' Home, the syllabus of the lecture on electric light, to which it had been a long promise that she should convey the party from the schoolroom on the morrow, her husband's rough memoranda for circulars of invitation to a drawing-room meeting on the subject of African missionary exploration, headings for an article in the *Sunday School Magazine!* Should she return to find these and sundry other documents quickened into life, and engaged in visible and rampant strife on the arena of her Davenport, such strife would but be an outward indication of the conflict of duties which seemed to Mrs. Stanton to be awaiting her equal and immediate attention.

"You are happy to be able so to dispose of your claims, Dr. Elwin. I am afraid I can hardly hope to do the same."

"My dear friend," was her host's calm reply, as, determinately *not* looking at his watch in a stand on the table, or at the list of engagements on his desk, or at the open Hebrew Bible, with headings for the next Sunday's sermon marking the page, he took up the question unexpectedly mooted, "If I believed in the possibility of 'conflicting duties,' I should give up my ministry as hopeless, and write underneath, 'Let all things be done decently and in order.' *Impossible*! Believe me, whether Solomon understood it or not, his prayer concerning '*the thing of a day in his day, as the matter shall require*,' had in it the very essence of New Testament life—the life of childlike following and reception. That, lived out, would effect a marvelous transformation in many a course which should exhibit, instead of a turmoil of so called 'conflicting duties,' 'peace flowing as a river' as its testimony to a perfect planning from on high.

"I think," he added, taking a paper from the table-drawer, and, after sealing it in an envelope, placing it in Mrs. Stanton's hand, "that, as we are such old friends, I must share with you some morning thoughts which have been of help to me. Will you open this to-morrow at that early service of consecration in which the new day is dedicated to God, a day during which we must recognize as a first principle His individual guidance covenanted for all that it may bring?"

Mrs. Stanton's thanks, as she received the envelope, were slightly mechanical— an under-current of practical difficulty occupying her thoughts as she recurred to Dr. Elwin's previous words.

"I suppose you have an especial gift of order,—far more than I,—and can arrange and reduce all your calls to system, so that they do not jostle each other like my homelier ones," she said thoughtfully.

"Apparently contending *calls*!" was the reply. "That is another matter! If I were to regard all so-styled calls as duties I should have to be at all points of the parish and at all departments of study at once— schools, superintendence of workers, visiting, Hebrew exegesis, and preparations for Bible classes claiming simultaneous attention, instead of my being here to thank Mrs. Stanton for her kind visit, and to finish it off by requesting her to help me in working out a problem capable of a practical and continuous solution. No, method and order are first-class servants for the arrangement of one's work, and the power of judicious deputation is a first- class officer; but there needs something behind—something which must be supplied from a higher source: power to discern the order in which claims are to be taken up and the point at which calls become duties. I delight in one of Cecil's wise utterances: '*The opportunity of doing a good work, and the ability to do it, constitute the call.*' If prior, God-sent duties, by full occupation of time and strength, make it impossible for me to take up fresh occupations without endangering my carrying out of first orders according to His will, these, however tempting, are not '*calls*' from Him. Both the opportunity and ability are lacking.

"Do you see that vine, Mrs. Stanton?" he continued. "I was thinking this morning, how manifold are its operations,— chemical analyses from soil and atmosphere, dispositions of its varied nutriments, the working up of the sap and sunshine into leafy clothing and fruit, the outbreathing of gaseous supplies as its component quota to the common atmosphere,—and yet, withal, what completeness in each department of its work! no one conflicting with any other in its fulfillment of a perfectly prearranged ordering!"

"It has a great deal to do, certainly," responded Mrs. Stanton in a practical voice, after following Dr. Elwin's illustration with the interest and reverence invariably devoted to his words, and mentally adapting his picture of vine-life to her own varied occupations; "but it has not to write sermons or manage a parish like you, Dr. Elwin; nor to see to children, and servants, and house, or to be in half a dozen places at once, like me."

Dr. Elwin smiled. "I do not know about writing sermons," he replied. "I should be thankful could I in the least emulate my vine-teacher in *preaching* them! It certainly has not to be in half a dozen places at once, nor have either of us; and the effort to achieve such ubiquity would unquestionably, in my case, spoil the work done at each one of any six specified stations."

Then gravely opening his Bible at the Epistle to the Ephesians, he read the words: "For we are His workmanship, created in Jesus

Christ for good works, which God afore prepared that we should walk in them."

"Long ago," he went on, "I was rigid in keeping to a time-table, framed, as I imagined, for the carrying on of self-discipline and active usefulness with the greatest possible effectiveness. The least irregularity in obedience to its calls served to chafe my spirit. So many hours to study, so many to parish visiting; so many to family calls; in fact, I regarded a close adherence to my own appointment of time as all-important.

"I had learned the first lesson of consecration: '*all for Christ*'; but I had not learned the next: 'All for Him *according to His ordering*.' Plans, system, mechanism are indeed as much a necessity for effectiveness in sustained Christian work as are the venous and capillary organizations of the plant; but all must be subservient to that higher ruling which does not come to us in supernatural revelations, but in the everyday duties and in the often prosaic, on-and-on occupations which are part of His individual arrangement who has said, 'In all thy ways acknowledge Him, and He shall direct thy paths.'

"He had to teach me that 'redeeming the time' could only be effected by my letting God's time-table supersede my own, by the recognition of His higher planning as put forth upon the stops as well as the steps—upon the hindrances as well as the calls; and by the discernment of His will in each so-called 'trifling' incident of everyday life.

"And as we get further the habit of childlike obedience should grow stronger. We should learn more and more *to look upon circumstances as providences*, and to realize the soul-communion maintained by a meeting of our thoughts with God's thoughts from moment to moment in the good works which He has prepared that we should walk in. He even now clasps the exercise of a submitted will with, 'If ye be willing and obedient, ye shall eat the good of the land'; and responds to 'As the eyes of servants look unto the hand of their masters, so our eyes wait upon the Lord,' with 'I will guide thee with Mine eye.' If we are but *in waiting*, He will show us that only one call at a time is really a *duty*; and He who organizes the ministry of 'angels that excel in strength, and that do His commandment, hearkening unto the voice of His word,' will give us, I increasingly believe, endowments of method and of organization which both multiply and economize power. But let us ever remember that the good works prepared are not let down from heaven in twos and threes, but just one by one in God's order. As we with faith and patience seek, day by day, to follow in the pathway of His plans,—to be 'of keen scent in the fear of the Lord,'—we shall know more and more of that secret communion, of that mutual 'pondering,' which belongs to our following them up according to His will, and to His glory."

Mrs. Stanton was silent. Dr. Elwin's words opened to her a momentary vista of calm and spirit-rest such as had never seemed to her within the range of possibility. Could this region of tranquility indeed be attained by the mother of eight children, a district visitor, a mistress of house and family, and an organizer of good works on all sides? The idea was dismissed from her vision as belonging to regions of transcendentalism which Dr. Elwin, in his study, and in the contemplation of his vine, might, perhaps, enjoy, and which, as "men don't understand," he could not be expected to recognize as impossible in her case.

He read her glance as she inquired, "But how are we always to know which, out of many, is the right duty and the first call? How can we be sure about what seem to be equal claims, or about those which, giving place to the 'ought' of the first, must be neglected?"

"Just as a devoted child will, in the course of loving obedience, get to know more and more of a father's mind. After we have accepted this individual ordering as a fact, as an unquestioned principle underlying the minutest decisions of everyday life, the spiritual habit of reading our Lord's guidance, and of discerning His order of precedence, becomes a second nature, changing the whole life from one of diffuse, even though of consecrated, aims, to one of most restful completeness. The intelligence which we put forth in regard to our ordinary affairs, the common-sense weighing of comparative claims, necessary to the most elementary arrangements of everyday duty, become, in this higher region of Christ-life, having for its incitement, 'The Father has not left me alone because I do always those things which please Him,' a keen spiritual insight. '*He is responsible*' becomes the heart's habitual resource concerning all *results* of God-guided decisions. Good-by, dear friend! may we both increasingly learn from Him—'the God that performeth all things for me'—happy secrets of life without worry, and work without friction!"

The shaking of hands was interrupted by a hurried knock at the study door; and, according to Mrs. Stanton's nomenclature, "a conflicting duty" presented itself in the shape of the servant with a hasty announcement, "If you please, sir, a message has come up from the hospital. John Hay, who met with a railway accident last week, is taken worse, and wants to see you once more. The house-surgeon says, could you please to come down directly?"

"At once, William,' was Dr. Elwin's reply; and, as Mrs. Stanton crossed to the door, the parting remark which greeted her ear was, "The order of precedence is quite clear in this case. My Sunday sermon and Hebrew Bible were not 'prepared for me to walk in' this morning, at all events."

Chapter II

IT was with grave thought that Mrs. Stanton wended her way in the June sunshine toward the Servants' Home, whither she had been summoned by a note from the matron whom she superintended. Was it to a beautiful theological essay that she had been listening? or was it to a revelation of a path of communion in common life—of rest in activity, of tranquillity in service—which lay before her now—immediately; and that, not as a matter of choice, but as the only true path of childlike following, and, consequently, the only path in which the peace and rest of birthright possession could possibly be realized?

"It would seem like being taken up every hour into God's confidence," she said to herself, "if, in my common, woman's life, I were to see His hand before me in the little things of the way, ordering every bit of it—if I were to look upon every day as a newly prepared gift, let down from Him to be lived out moment by moment according to his previous planning. One feels one's self so far down— one's little hourly comings and goings so insignificant; and yet—and yet—" and just as Mrs. Stanton rang the bell at the door of the neatly kept Home, the words flashed back to her mind which she had read before leaving her room that morning, "Ye have not chosen Me, but I have chosen you, and ordained you, that ye should go and bring forth fruit, and that your fruit should remain; that whatsoever ye shall ask of the Father in my name, He may give it you."

"Does not this mean far more of intimacy, far more of union and of fruit-bearing," she said to herself, "than I have ever fathomed or even attempted to fathom? I believe all that Dr. Elwin has been saying lies here, if only I could see to read and live it out more clearly."

The reason of her summons was communicated by the matron, as she took her seat in the little parlor whence a kindly jurisdiction had long been exercised, having influence on the life of many a young servant, who had gone forth from the well- ordered Home, helped and strengthened for trial and duty.

"It is about Mary Annis that I wish to speak to you, ma'am," said the matron; "and as the lady that was asking about her character said she would call at one o'clock to-day, and that she would be willing to take her on your recommendation,—her last mistress refusing to say more for her than 'honest, steady, and sober,'—I thought I had better let you know directly, as the poor girl might not get another chance."

"I cannot understand why it is that Mary does not keep her situations," said Mrs. Stanton; "she is a modest, truthful girl, very clever in work, and of a good respectable family. I have known her from the infant school upward, and, so far as I can judge, she is most willing and obliging."

"Willing enough, ma'am," was the reply, "but it seems to me that it is just there that the fault is, or rather, the danger. have had her as my own servant this week; and it really vexes me to see a good housemaid— or, at least, one that has the making of a good housemaid—going to waste, so to speak, for want of knowing how to do what she is told. It is really only that with Mary. She is willing enough to obey orders in a general way; but whether she has been under mistresses that have set her to do more than she could manage, or whether she has got into a notion that she can order best for herself, I don't know. There it is, anyhow: she can't go on in a steady round like any well-trained girl, but must take up first this, then that, out of her own head; and then she gets fussed and worried because things are not done in time, bringing discredit, as if she were overworked, on those above her. Day after day it is the same. There is always a sort of hurry and unfinishedness, making her feel—and me too—as if the work was never done and never could be. Only yesterday I gave her the orders for turning out this room, and for cleaning it thoroughly. She knows how to do it as well as I do, and went to it with a real willingness and interest, which were a pleasure to see. Well, I thought that the chairs had been out in the hall a long time, and that, while I was training in a new hand at the cooking, things seemed very quiet overhead; so I came upstairs to see what was going on. Well, ma'am, there was Mary as busy as possible. She had hardly given the first rub to the windows, but I found her with the watering can and scissors, at work over those plants in the boxes, and clipping at the ivy round the windows.

"'O Mrs. Hughes!' she said quite pleasantly, 'I wish you had waited only a little bit longer! I had set my mind on getting these trimmed up, and the old leaves cleared away before you came.'

"'That is all very fine, Mary,' I answered; 'but I didn't tell you to look to the flower boxes, which my lame niece makes it her pride to come across and see to herself, and, what is more, does not like anyone else meddling with. Your work was to clean out this room, and I don't see that it is half, or half a quarter done. Why, what's this laid out on the shelf? What's the meaning of all this litter of paper?'

"'You wasn't to see it till it was put up,' said my head servant, with quite a cheeriness in her voice. 'I thought I'd cut out a fire ornament for your parlor, like what my mistress was making for hers when I came away; only it took longer than I expected.'

"'Now listen, Mary,' I said; 'when I tell you to clean out a room round by flower boxes and fire ornaments, it will be time enough for you to take to that way of housework; and, meantime, as you know quite well where the course of your duty lies,—the lifting out and covering up, and tea-leaves sweeping, and paint washing, window cleaning, and rubbing up with the polish, which you won't get in many houses besides this,—you will please to work my way and not your own, and not to go upon "I thought you would like," instead of attending to the works to which you are called, and the plain duties which are yours to do in the order in which I have told you to do them."'

Mrs. Hughes paused. "As I said, ma'am, she's a nice girl. It's not *willingness* that is wanting, but the willingness, so to speak, in harness. Yesterday, it seemed as if this room, which didn't want two hours for thorough doing out, was never to be finished. I answered the door myself in the afternoon, for she was not much more than dressed by tea-time. had promised the girls that, if their work was done in good time, they should go to the Missionary Dissolving-views at the schoolhouse in the evening, and it was a real trouble to me to keep Mary back; but I knew it was a good lesson for her that she should do the needlework after tea, which ought to have been finished by five o'clock. As I said to her, 'My dear, it's a common saying, "Where there's a will there is a way"; but with you it's the other thing; you've got the will, but you want to do it after your own way, instead of that which is put right before you to follow out. Look up in the sky. The sun goes on doing his work, and has nothing to say to the moon or to the stars. That is not his business, which is to light the world by day, the moon doing the same by night. So all work in order, and that's how it is brought down to us in poetry, as you have often said:

"'Oh like the sun may I fulfill
The appointed duties of the day,
With ready mind and active will
March on, and keep my heavenly way.'"

"Well, Mrs. Hughes," interposed Mrs. Stanton, not pausing to question the scientific accuracy of her illustration, "I am glad you have given Mary a good lesson on the subject; and now, what about the situation that has opened for her?"

"Well, ma'am, Mrs. Burnside is just the mistress for Mary. She's firm and she's kind and she's just; and she gives her thought to each of her servants' work as, perhaps, a mistress in a larger house couldn't. She plans it all out for them beforehand, and lets them know that what they have got to do is to work out in her plans, not in their own. She does not expect them to be in half a dozen places at once "—a vivid reminiscence of her observation to Dr. Elwin not an hour before came to Mrs. Stanton's mind—"and she lets them feel she trusts them (and that is what Mary is worthy of feeling), so that they get to strive to please from knowing and loving, both. I'd like Mary to get this place. I told Mrs. Burnside about her faults; and she said that, considering we thought well of her character and her willingness and truth, if you would recommend her as what you really considered suitable for the place, she would give her a trial. She would want her to-morrow, her own housemaid having been called away suddenly to a dying mother. I said that I felt sure you would do your best for her."

"That I most certainly will," was the answer; and before the writing of the note which was to decide her fate, Mary was summoned for a private interview with Mrs. Stanton, who, after some kindly counsel pressing home the matron's advice, closed with the words, "And now, Mary, remember—let us both remember"—and, if Mary had known the truth, a freshly roused remembrance of her interview with Dr. Elwin lay behind the inclusive clause in Mrs. Stanton's valediction, "that there is often as much self-will in wanting to do our earthly master's work, as well as our heavenly Master's, in our own way, as in wanting to choose our own way altogether. It is not work for Him, if He has not put it for us to do."

And then, going to her own private drawer, Mrs. Stanton took out a neat illuminated card, with a bright ribbon suspender, and with the inscription:

"Lord, what wilt Thou have me to do?"

As she gave it to the girl, whose eyes moistened, partly at the kindly touch of the hand on her shoulder, and partly with a sense of the motherly sympathy with which her prospects and character were regarded by her friend, she added, "There, dear child; put that up over your bedside, and every morning ask God to let you see His ordering for the day in the orders of the master and mistress whom He has placed over you. And ask Him to enable you to do all—even the smallest things— from the one motive of love to Him who gave His life for you."

* * * * * * *

"I wonder whether Mary in the least suspected that, while my little sermon was addressed to her, it was far more spoken to myself?" thought Mrs. Stanton, as she walked up the shady avenue of chestnuts which brought her to her own door.

"It seems to me as if I had passed through an education since I went out this morning; as if a wholly new view of life had come to me; as if I must get time to sort my ideas of service in a perfectly different light from that of three hours ago. I should like to write down every word spoken by Dr. Elwin of 'life without worry, work without friction.' He does not speak lightly, and he meant what he said. Much as I generally miss them, I am glad the schoolroom party are out for the day, so that I may think it all over by myself."

An unusual quiet reigned in the house. The young people, with their governess, were celebrating a birthday by a long- promised expedition to a friend's park at a distance. The two nursery vassals, not yet awakened from their before-dinner sleep, demanded no attention; and, after a quiet visit to the chamber in which they lay, Mrs. Stanton descended to her morning room. Everything was as she had left it. The papers on her Davenport had not been disturbed, and for several minutes after taking her usual seat, she refrained from laying a finger on them. By some only partially defined association they—lying there in their confusion—had in her eyes assumed a representative character. Indistinctly she regarded them as associated in testimony concerning her life—a life of service, indeed, and that loving service, but yet marred by a hurry and unrest of which it seemed to her that she had for the first time become vividly conscious.

With a sudden linking of thought there came to her mind a remembrance of the old fairy story of her childhood, in which a crowd of well-meaning efforts, involved in hopeless confusion as the result of Disorder's entanglements, were in a moment directed into clear, definite channels by that touch of the fairy Order's wand, which, with magic power, sorted and arranged for harmonious onworking all that before was chaos.

Had not her spiritual vision received some such magic touch? Had not the life clew which she had hitherto failed to grasp been presented to her in words which she had known from her childhood, but which, as an every-day working power, had been in her arrangements practically a dead letter?

She opened her Bible at the Epistle to the Ephesians. The first words on which she lighted stood out with a fresh force of meaning: "Be ye not unwise, but understanding what the will of the Lord is."

"How well I knew what good advice was suitable for Mary Annis' case! But has not her mistake been mine? Have not I been struggling to grasp much outer service, telling myself that I was doing His will, while I have seldom stopped still to inquire whether this crowding of work was indeed the will of God in Christ Jesus concerning me? Is it too late to acquire the habit? Have I so accustomed myself to regard work and service as identical, as to have failed to seek the quick discernment for God's guidance, which, as Dr. Elwin said, is a primary requisite in working it out?"

She turned to the words which he had quoted, "*Good works which God afore prepared that we should walk in them*!" "These carried out would make my life a perfectly new existence. Are they, as he said, really and truly there for me to put in practice at this moment? May I believe that as actually as our own children in their schoolroom fill up, from day to day, the plans which their parents have prepared for them to follow, I may, in my own everyday life, work out my Father's prearranged time-table for me, and meet His thoughts and ordering at every turn? How much closer it would make my intimacy with Him! How the love- surprises belonging to 'I being in the way, the Lord led me,' would strengthen faith!"

Then Mrs. Stanton, falling into a brief train of thought, traveled back to a memory of her girlhood. Unexpectedly a long journey across country, to Scotland, from the house in which she had been visiting, had to be undertaken without the escort in those days deemed necessary for a properly protected young lady. "How my father's love was before me in the way!" she thought. "I remember as if it were yesterday, how, at this change of train, at that stopping-place on the journey, some friend met me, some greeting unexpectedly encountered me—all the result of his tender forethought, which, without my knowledge, had planned surprises of care throughout the way. And every bit of my pilgrim-life would, according to these words, bring to light such indications of Fatherly prevision and love, if only the discerning might be granted. More than this, the communion of love and gratitude which with the earthly father could only be maintained by letter from a distance, would with the heavenly Father be a conscious and continued intercourse. Each good work before prepared for me to walk in would seem like a new station of actual soul-to soul meeting with my Lord Himself.

"But then, am I ready for this walk? *Am I willing*? For there must be a giving up, as well as a receiving. I see in a moment that I have tried, like Mary Annis with her flower boxes and fire ornaments, concerning which Mrs. Hughes descanted so eloquently, to grasp more work than I can do unhurriedly and with due regard to home duties which, for me, come clearly as God's first ordering. Shall I be satisfied to see a portion of my district work handed over to another? to depute, possibly, more than one of my classes to those who, with fewer home claims, can carry them on more at leisure? to give up many a pleasant bit of magazine authorship for the every-day correspondence which has a first claim on my time, and, still more, for deeper study of God's Word, not only as a teacher of others, but as a hungry learner for myself? I asked Dr. Elwin how I was to be sure of the order of precedence among varied claims. I believe that what he said was true, and that there can be no real discerning what the will of the Lord is until our own will is not only theoretically, but truly, submitted to His. It is all in those words, 'My sheep hear My voice, and I know them, and they follow Me'; and—there comes the question—has my will been really surrendered to that of my Lord?"

Kind reader of these pages, no one more strongly than their writer would deprecate the introduction into fictitious narrative of the solemnities of prayer and communion with God. But, with the assurance that a slight drapery of imaginary surroundings here veils a narrative of real life, its next incident may be safely recorded. With the deep earnestness belonging to a conscious taking-up of her whole life on a new basis and with the heart-cry "Rabboni, Master!" Mrs. Stanton placed her finger on the page before her, uttering the lowly prayer, "Teach me all this—any way—how Thou pleasest—only in Thine own way! Let me never miss a blessing through my refusal to see Thine ordering Hand! Let me never lose one of Thy confidences of love and guidance because of my dullness to discern the smallest or humblest good work, whether of doing or of waiting, of effort or of suffering, which Thou hast prepared for me to walk in! Now—now, as never before—behold the handmaid of the Lord: be it unto me according to Thy word!"

Chapter III

IT was evening. Mr. Stanton had come home from the bank in which he was a partner. The young people had returned from their excursion. What difference— felt, rather than seen—marked the aspect of the wife and mother, betraying itself in the gladness of her greetings, and in the disengaged sympathy with which she listened to her husband's report of the day's work, and to her children's recital of what she truly termed their "bank-holiday enjoyments." Descriptions of wanderings on Helstone Ridge, and of tea out of doors on the hillside, and of the gathering of flower trophies brought home in triumph, were poured forth on a ready ear. Something indefinable, but something very real, had come to her life. Unconsciously to herself she had begun to tread that higher track of living communion for which, till now, room had not been found in a life of lower level, of less stillness of soul.

Admission to "late dinner" was a clause in the Magna Charta of birthday privileges rigidly maintained amongst the young people of West View Lodge.

"And as it is Harry's birthday, papa has promised to read to us this evening," exclaimed two of the girls joyously, as, through the flowery hall, the whole party passed to the drawing-room.

"Mother, you will not be too busy, will you, to sit with us? Nothing is half the pleasure when we see you away at that Davenport writing, writing, and when you have no time to enjoy things with us. Besides, you ought not to work so hard; you want a holiday sometimes."

"Too busy, my child: certainly not!" was the answer. "I cleared off plenty of work while you were all on Helstone Ridge, and put away for to-morrow all that could not be managed to-day, so that I may have a happy time with my dear ones to-night."

If the chorus of gladness at this announcement fell upon Mrs. Stanton's ear with a private echo of self-reproach, as she looked back upon evenings during which "too busy" had often been her regretful reply to similar appeals, no shadow of trouble now appeared on her brow; and it would have been hard to imagine a more joyous family group than that gathered in the drawing-room, as her husband produced the volume from which, with especial reference to Harry's taste, he had selected passages for the evening's reading.

They were taken from an old story of "Life amongst the North American Indians," and gave a vivid description of the long following up of a trail in pursuit of a captured heroine. Mr. Stanton was an admirable reader, and the children kindled into breathless eagerness as Hawk Eye's dexterity, and the almost miraculous acuteness of his Indian companions in detecting the track of the fugitives, were depicted. Through woods, across prairies, the pursuit was conducted; a broken twig here, a crushed flower there, sufficiently indicating to their practiced eyes the course they had taken. Now a blind—an effort to put the pursuer on a false track—was brought to light. Now an almost imperceptible disturbance of the sand beside the stream told of a crossing adroitly conducted. Now an apparent absence of any indication befell the search until some almost imperceptible token of passage gave a clue. And so, after days and weeks spent in an undaunted following up of the trail, the end was reached, and the concluding capture and catastrophe brought forth loud exclamations of interest and admiration from Mr. Stanton's audience.

Pleasant chat and games followed, while, in Mrs. Stanton's mind, an undercurrent of thought connected the morning's tide of reflection with the children's evening reading. "On the trail!" The words associated themselves with other words: "Good works afore prepared for them to walk in." Was not the North American story, chosen for Harry's delectation, in truth a parable of deepest meaning for his mother? The closely exercised discernment, the acuteness of detection, exhibited by these children of the wilds, might they not have their translation in that "keen scent in the fear of the Lord," of which Dr. Elwin had spoken to her? Might they not have their New Testament transposition in that "discerning what the will of the Lord is," which, as never before, she had seen to be the true vocation of the redeemed? Would not common days become holy days, if, *in* the homely calls to ordinary duties, the necessary visits, the business notes and accounts, the claims for spiritual and temporal ministry, she might, even as those pursuers in the bent flower and broken twig—only with an absolute and love-quickened certainty—trace indications of the Hand before her in the way "prepared" for her and for her alone?

"*On the Trail!*" It was with the throb of something like new life that she repeated the words to herself. Oh, for the joy, day by day, of continually reading these indications of Fatherly preparation! Oh, for the love and obedience which should prevent her from ever losing sight of the clew in the covenant path ordered in all things and sure!

The words of the old sweet hymn, always sung at evening prayers on birthday occasions, chimed in with her thoughts:

"Guide me, O Thou Great Jehovah,
  Pilgrim through this barren land;
I am weak, but Thou art mighty,
  Lead me by Thy powerful Hand!
Strong Deliverer,
  Only by Thy help I stand!"

Had she ever sung that hymn as now? Had not a vague classification of its petitions into a general desire for direction and protection through life been the limit of the thoughts which had found their expression in its words?

Her husband's voice in the first verse of the twenty-fifth psalm, "Unto Thee, O Lord, do I lift up my soul," roused her from her inquiry. Had that psalm been in God's Word for her all along? Was it not from some hitherto unknown Revised Version that he was reading? Almost unconsciously she took up the Bible which lay by her side as if to satisfy herself, as promise met prayer, and assurance clasped entreaty: "Show me Thy ways, O Lord; teach me Thy paths! Lead me in Thy truth, and teach me: for Thou art the God of my salvation; on Thee do I wait all the day...

Good and upright is the Lord: therefore will He teach sinners in the way. The meek will He guide in judgment: and the meek will He teach His way... All the paths of the Lord are mercy and truth unto such as keep His covenant and His testimonies... The secret of the Lord is with them that fear Him: and He will show them His covenant."

And this was for her. No new psalm! no new teaching! Only the high call, to be one of God's souls in waiting, had come to her as never before. Hence-forth, and for always, she realized that when He said, "The secret of the Lord is with them that fear Him," He meant it.

* * * * * * *

Early the next morning Mrs. Stanton opened the envelope which, before parting, Dr. Elwin had placed in her hand, and read as follows:

Early Service

"We are His workmanship, created in Christ Jesus for good works, which God afore prepared that we should walk in them." — Eph. ii. 10. "His way is perfect."

Be still, O waking soul!
  Now, from the courts of heaven,
With early dew of "mercies new"
  Another day is given.
Fenced off from fields of time—
  Its span a holy rood—
Unsullied see descend for thee
  A day prepared by God.

A day prepared by God!
  Mine freshly from His hand!
Oh! through the hours, for quickened powers
  His will to understand!
Be mine the listening heart!
  Be mine the sight renewed!
Be mine the grace His plans to trace
  With thought and will subdued!

Father, the day is Thine;
  Framed with minutest care;
In need foreseen let love serene
  Prevent me everywhere!
Guide, lest through erring sight,
  Through dull or clouded sense,
One touch I miss of heaven's own bliss
  In Thy deep confidence.

I journey forth to-day,
  A track unknown to explore,
A sacred path revealed to Faith
  Of works "prepared before."

Linked to occasion's call,
Her Heaven-taught eye shall see
With claims intwined, in toil enshrined,
A secret "Unto ME!"

Grant me in hourly charge
Thine ordinance to trace!
Obeyed by love, its task shall prove
A sacrament of grace.
Let me on toilsome steep
But mark with vision sure
Thy guiding clew, and gladness new
Shall quicken to endure.

The weary and the sad,
As messengers from Thee
Bid me discern, and lowly learn
In them the Christ to see.
On possible emprise,
In many a secret call
Of silent need, oh, let me read
Thine own sign-manual!

What though grief's torrent wild
Invade my path to-day?
'Twas by this ford went forth my Lord,
His footprints mark the way.
What if those footprints lead
By valley-path of pain?
Whisper for me "*Gethsemane*!"
And suffering shall be gain.

What though alone, alone
Thou bid me stand and wait
While calls resound and needs abound
Beyond the fast-closed gate;
Perchance pavilion royal
Shall canopy my road,
Which shall be found thrice holy ground
Of audience with God.

A day prepared by Thee!
  Father, Thy way be mine!
That I may trace soul-meeting place—
  Love's hidden countersign—
In joys, in homeliest cares,
  In wayside communing,
Thus raised by Thee to high degree
  As service for the King.

Then, when the shadows fall,
  And I resign my trust,
And the finished day shall pass away
  To the Holy and the Just,
Father, forgive! forgive!
  Sprinkle with cleansing blood
Ere Thou with sleep grant earnest deep
  Of rest prepared with God.

* * * * * * *

On the following Sunday Dr. Elwin preached from Isaiah xl. "The sermon which I interrupted!" thought Mrs. Stanton to herself, as he gave out the text. "But how much do I owe to his looking on my visit, not as an interruption, but as a call!"

His subject carried on the train of thought which, for her, had begun beside the open Bible in his study; and his summing up, as he read the whole passage, gave a new indorsement to his teaching.

"'To whom then will ye liken me, or shall I be equal? saith the Holy One. Lift up your eyes on high, and behold who hath created these things, that bringeth out their host by number: He calleth them all by names, by the greatness of His might, for that He is strong in power; not one faileth. Why sayest thou, O Jacob, and speakest, O Israel, My way is hid from the Lord, and my judgment is passed over from my God? Hast thou not known? hast thou not heard, that the everlasting God, the Lord, the Creator of the ends of the earth, fainteth not, neither is weary? there is no searching of His understanding. He giveth power to the faint: and to them that have no might He increaseth strength. Even the youths shall faint and be weary, and the young men shall utterly fall. But they that wait upon the Lord shall renew their strength; they shall mount up with wings as eagles; they shall run and not be weary; and they shall walk and not faint.'

"Therefore remember—you who would know the rest in service which this passage should establish for you—that God's infinity as your Creator demands, as He Himself here stoops to explain to us, infinite minuteness in the ordering of every detail of your daily lives. You who, from deepest sense of your own unworthiness, are inclined to exclaim, 'My way is hid from the Lord, the knowledge of me is passed over from my God—I am too low down, too insignificant to claim His individual care and thought'—see in the glories of the orbs above you, the pledges of planning and guidance which touch your smallest actions, and what you might be inclined to call the most trivial incidents of your lives. Remember that it is not only that the Love witnessed by the gift of His Son pledges itself to shape your life for your great blessedness and for His glory. Were it possible for this love to be left out, *the attributes of the God of the universe demand it.* No way too lowly, no path too obscure, to be of importance in His sight

"'Who gives its lustre to an insect's wing,
And wheels His throne upon the rolling worlds.'

"But write across the life of the weakest and humblest in this congregation the one word '*redeemed,*' and what does that involve on the part of the God and Father of our Lord Jesus Christ? He, the Son, knew, as the strife approached, and the '*Nevertheless*' was to be spoken on which hung the weight of the whole world's redemption, all that His disciples would need of assurance concerning an ever-present love and a never-dying companionship.

"'Jesus answered and said, If a man love Me, he will keep my words; and My Father will love him, and *We* will come unto him, and make Our abode with him.'

"Dear brother or sister, fearful of claiming too much of your Father's minute attention, deeming yourself unworthy to grasp this individual, personal care and ordering, seek rather to glorify Him *by claiming up to these words*, by rising to the height of your charter, by learning, as stargazers of old were exhorted to learn on the plains of Chaldea, that your individual covenant reaches to the heavens, and is inscribed in God's own handwriting on our midnight sky:

"'The voice which rolls the stars along
Spake all the promises.'"

CHAPTER IV

FROM that week Mrs. Stanton's was a changed life. More listening, less struggling; less attempted, more effected; a communion sustained, rather than interrupted, by every-day calls and occupations; outer work often abridged that soul- work might have room; the current of life deepened rather than widened; rest found *in* service, as well as rest received *for* service; the peace *of* God entered into as an inheritance having for its title-deed peace *with* God; sickness and suffering— and such came to her life—solemnly recognized as part of His plan, and, consequently, not as a break in service, but as a call to higher service; bereavement, as well as enrichment, accepted as by one admitted to the Bethany confidences of resurrection-life, and deciphered as those alone can decipher the teachings of grief who own the key of love's submitted will.

"How many a false estimate of work and service had to be forever abandoned!" she wrote in her diary, years after, on the anniversary of that June morning on which our narrative opens. "How great the love which could sprinkle with the blood of an undying atonement the accumulated work in which there had been so much of self, so little of surrender! How continually do I need that sprinkling still, as every fresh view of the beauty of His guidance condemns my own imperfect following, '*On the trail*' has ever since that time had for me a meaning which no one would guess who did not know my history! I had, indeed, in theory and, to a certain degree, in reality, adopted the life of my Lord and Master as my accepted example; but how little had I realized the privilege of following His steps moment by moment in a communion of good works prepared by His love for me to walk in!

"I think those words became, on that day, an epitaph written up over the grave of my 'conflicting duties!'"

"When The King Comes To His Own!"

IT was a glorious summer evening; and as, through the glades and meadow land of Kent, an eastward bound train traveled on in somewhat leisurely fashion, its passengers beheld a sunset which might well call forth exclamations of admiration, while banner clouds of crimson and gold ranged themselves in the western sky as for a farewell triumph.

"What will it be when the King comes!"

The words were spoken half to herself, half to a young lady in the same carriage, by a traveler in mourning, whose face had caught the glow of the sunset, and who, from gazing into the glory-chambers, turned to share with her fellow-passenger the admiration which she felt must be kindled by the spectacle.

"What will it be when the King comes!" she repeated more earnestly, observing the look of hesitation with which her remark was received; "does not a sunset like this make you wonder what that Coming will be?"

"I really cannot tell of whom you are speaking," was the answer, after a moment's pause, in which the person addressed seemed to be puzzled as to whether the carriage was shared with some disloyal subject of Queen Victoria, secretly or openly attached to a rival cause.

"Behold He cometh with clouds, and every eye shall see Him!" was the answer given in grave and gentle tones. "Surely you are looking forward to that Coming?" and in so kindly a manner was the question presented that silence was impossible.

"I can't say that it is a subject I ever think about," was the reply, honestly, if somewhat coldly, made.

"*But He is our King*: He is coming, and coming soon, as surely as that sun will rise again to-morrow—coming in the clouds of heaven—coming with the crown of life for those who love His appearing. Surely you will not look upon that 'blessed hope' as no concern of yours," pleaded the elder lady—and the train slackened speed, a rural station was reached, and, seemingly with a sense of relief, the traveler so unexpectedly addressed alighted on the platform.

The brief conversation was at an end. "A subject that I do not think about!" The words came back sadly on the ear. "Come, Lord

Jesus, come quickly!" was the heart- cry which alone seemed to harmonize with the sunset vision: a cry for

"The joy of the Christmas morning
When the King shall meet His own!"

"When the King comes to His own!" Let us travel back from summer sunshine, and from Kentish cherry orchards—from hop gardens and river meadows—to wintry fogs and city smoke, even to the birthplace of the words in the hour of sunset foretelling a Coming which for one meant nothing, for another, *all*.

It was not exactly a whisper that I heard one winter's evening as Christmas was nearing, I will not say how long ago, in a song coming out of a little room in a London street. It was not a grand room in any sense, and in it there had been sorrow and sickness. The voice, which once was as clear and strong as the bravest for singing out "*Hark, the herald angels*" in the church choir, was so weak and trembling that you would hardly have called its notes "singing." But the words—the words had such a triumph in them that you would have said that it was a song of soldiers looking on to victory. Let me pause here to write it down—the song which came out of the fog and smoke, the song with the Christmas ring in it, and which I have never forgotten since:

"I hear the sob of the parted,
The wail of the broken-hearted,
The sigh for the love departed
In the surging roar of the town.
And it's oh for the joy of the Morning!
The light and song of the Morning!
There'll be joy in the Christmas Morning
When the King comes to His own!

"Now let our hearts be true, brothers,
To suffer and to do, brothers;
There'll be a song for you, brothers,
When the battle's fought and won.
It won't seem long in the Morning,
In the light and song of the Morning;
There'll be joy in the Christmas Morning
When the King comes to His own!

"Arise, and be of good cheer, brothers;
The day will soon be here, brothers;
The victory is near, brothers;
    And the sound of the glad 'Well done!'
There'll be no sad heart in the Morning;
No tear will start in the Morning;
There'll be joy in the Christmas Morning
    When the King comes to His own!

We're in for the winning side, brothers,
Bound to the Lord who died, brothers,
We shall see Him glorified, brothers,
    And the Lamb shall wear the crown.
What of the cold world's scorning?
There'll be joy enough in the Morning—
There'll be joy in the Christmas Morning
    When the King comes to His own!"

That was the Christmas battle-song that stirred my heart. A little child must have been in the room, for I caught an almost baby-voice taking up the words, "*There'll be joy in the Christmas Morning,*" as the tune, which I had never heard anywhere else, died out; and you will believe me that I went my way with the words ringing in my ears—yes, ringing like Christmas bells:

"There'll be joy in the Christmas Morning
    When the King comes to His own!"

Well, of course these words set me thinking just as they would have set you thinking. What about this second Christmas that is nearing? What about this King coming to His own? Does it all mean anything? Is there anything real in it? You couldn't go up one street and down another, the Christmas twilight shading down into the darkness, and those words sounding on in your ears, without putting the question to yourself which I put to myself: "Do the people here in this world of ours believe anything about this thing really—before very long, perhaps—coming to pass, about the joy of a Christmas Morning when the King *shall* come to His own? *And what will that Coming be to me?*"

Now, I may as well tell you at once that my work has led me in and out of a good many homes; and it strikes me that you might be willing to look in with me here and there, and to see what a difference it is making to some of our fellow men and women in their work in the world to think that the day is drawing nearer and nearer when the King, who says, "Behold, I come quickly," *will* come to His own.

Look in at this house. There is a hardworking mother here. You see what a struggling place it is, what a struggling life hers is. There is little of what the songs about Christmas fare tell of; for the breadwinner has been laid up in hospital for many a week, and to keep body and soul together is pretty much all that can be done for the children. The little ones are asleep at last, their bits of holly and ivy set out over the mantel-piece, so that even in that poor home there is something to remind us that Christmas has come round; and their mother gets ready for the night, and sees to the food for the next day's breakfast, before she sits down by the few coals of fire for a moment's rest.

Hark! there are the Christmas bells ringing out! Hark! there are the carol singers! "A merry Christmas!" It doesn't seem much like a "merry Christmas" in that poor room, does it? But what about it's being a *happy* one? There is a sort of happiness—the kind that I care to go in for—without any electroplate about it. You may rub and rub silver that is true metal all through, and it will only shine the brighter, and that is just how it is with the joy which no man taketh from you.

Do you see the poor mother's eyes brighten as she catches sight of the text round which the little ones have wreathed their holly? What are the words?

"He shall appear to your joy."

I know her well enough to put her thoughts into words as she takes down the Bible from the shelf to read the old good news brought by the angels to the shepherds: "Yes, He will come again, and He will know me, and I shall see His face— the One who has been my Friend in all the hard times here. With Him the troubles have not ever seemed troubles with the sting in them. He has taken the heavy end for me; and 'Cast thy burden on the Lord' has been His own word for the weary and heavy-laden. When I see Him I'll remind Him of the times He's brought me through; I'll remind Him of the illness from which He raised me up, and of the temptations to doubt His love which He shined away out of my soul by His Holy Spirit. *He'll* remember, I'm sure of that! He won't have forgotten all the burdens He's borne for us, all the care for the mother with the children. I'll thank Him then as I can't thank Him now. I'll trust Him now—now in the struggle—as I'll trust Him then when He comes to victory. Yes, because Thou hast been my help, therefore under the shadow of Thy wings will I rejoice."

Come away with me, my friend. We have other places to visit before we wish each other "Good-by." At all events, in one poor house you can catch something like a fresh whisper of the song of which I was writing to you:

"There'll be joy in the Christmas Morning
When the King comes to His own!"

But here we pause before a large building of many windows. Hospital? union? infirmary? Which is it? standing, as it does, like an island of strength and solidity in the midst of a sea of city tumult and surging life. Up stone stairs, along corridors, past wards—one so like another that we wonder how people who dwell in them know how to find their way without mistake. There are Christmas banners with which many are busying themselves. "ON EARTH PEACE!" glitters forth in silver letters at the end of one passage. "A HAPPY NEW YEAR" flutters against the wall on a flag, half hiding with its folds a door, on which as we enter we read, "MASTER'S ROOM."

A busy room it seems! You would at first sight say that Christmas Eve has come to its occupants in plain clothes, so to speak—as the 24th of December, and nothing more; for, except that Christmas has sent up his card in the form of a sprig of holly which has found its way to the mantel-shelf, and that many parcels are about, registers and account-books seem to engross the attention of the busy middle- aged man at the desk near the window. He looks up as a door on the opposite side of the room admits a pleasant-faced, strongly built woman, who, with a sickly child in her arms, seats herself near the fire as for a moment's rest.

"Nearly finished?" inquires the man at the desk.

"Getting on," is the reply; "I do believe that at last all the nurses have their orders, their presents for the wards, and the Christmas

Letters for the patients; and you've seen to the other side of the house. There seems a deal to do, and yet, by giving out so much in charge to each one, and taking time to see that they all know their work, I believe we are pretty nearly through for to-morrow."

"And that baby?"

"Poor little dear; it cried after me so! and its mother only died a week ago! So I brought it away for a bit of mothering by the fire here. Some one'll be coming for it after a little." And the said two-year-old infant, slowly consuming a biscuit from a box apparently kept on the shelf for use on such occasions, looked solemnly into the fire from its temporary home in the mistress' lap, as if trying to find in the red coals some secret information as to the life on which it had somewhat sadly started.

"Did you look in at the chapel?"

"Yes, for a minute: they're busy there. The chaplain's sent down a scroll for under the window. It's different from any they have had before; just the words:

"'I WILL COME AGAIN!'

and, underneath:

"'LOOKING FOR THAT GLORIOUS APPEARING.'"

"It's wonderful to think that's true. Somehow folks seem to go on as if it meant nothing. It seemed to me, as I went through the wards after looking in, and reading those words to myself, as if——"

"Well?"

"Why, as if—if we all out and out believed it in our lives, as we say we do with our lips——"

"That everything would have to set itself to that," resumed her husband, still bending over his desk.

"Exactly; you always know how to put my thoughts into words, William. *Do we believe it?*"

"'*Who shall come again.*' We say it twice every Sunday at chapel," was the reply; and the master ruled the closing line in the register, shut his book, and, leaning forward, paused for a moment, as if silently thinking over his wife's words while he rested from his labor.

"We seem to work so hard, Christmas after Christmas, to get things bright for the wards," she continued; "but somehow the thought of that other Christmas on in front—which will come we don't know how soon—well, don't we seem to shut it up in the Prayer Book between Sundays? I don't fancy that I'm looking for it as if it was real—as if—as if—you were going out to India, William, and I was looking out for you, and counting the days for you to come back."

"I've had my thoughts about it all, many a time," is the reply. "Suppose we were to put that 'looking for the Coming' into all our lives, mother, wouldn't it be something like for the New Year? We're taken up a deal, as is right, with keeping all straight for the Board and for the credit of the House: it would lift everything up a bit higher if 'looking for the King' went into all! "And the door was suddenly blown open by a gust of wind, which brought to the "Master's room" the sound of voices in the chapel adjoining, where the singers were practicing the hymns for the morrow:

"Oh that with yonder sacred throng
We at His feet may fall;
Join in the everlasting song,
And crown Him Lord of all!"

"If that means anything it means everything," he continued, after a moment's pause; "and—there's the question again— *Do* we believe it?"

"Do we believe it?" It is time we should leave the wards and courts of the vast city workhouse where the song of the second Christmas—of the crowning of the Coming King—meets the celebrations of the first Coming "in great humility." Some hearts are there, at all events, to which the glowing thought has come that every day may be glorified, and burdens lightened, and toil uplifted into high service by the blessed hope of

"Joy in the Christmas morning,
When the King comes to His own!"

We are at the West End now, among the grand houses in which poverty and empty grates are unknown. Look at this large mansion. The masters have been away in the country, but the family returns to-night. The servants have been busy making all things ready for the home-coming. They have been up early, and, as you see by the lights from the windows, are working still. A livery servant has come to the steps, and looks out in the direction from which the carriage may be expected. He is joined by a young woman, who gives a final polish to the brasses of the hall-door, the bell-handles, and the letter-box, and then, her task completed, stands for a moment by his side. You can see from their likeness to each other that they are brother and sister. They have been for many a day in the same service, that of the master on whose country estate they were born and brought up, and in whose employment they have risen to be trusted with a trust which, to a true and faithful servant, is of untold price.

"The Christmas bells, John!" exclaims the sister. "Don't they seem to take us home? They're ringing in Christmas there! If only we could hear them! It's almost time now, isn't it?"

"We'll see the carriage in a minute," was the reply. "Are you all finished up, Mary?"

"All—every bit—from kitchen to attic, John. Isn't it good getting ready for the coming back at Christmas? It puts such a spirit into one's work when it's for masters one loves to get back—and our master and mistress are so quick to see when we've taken pains to please them. Though it's no more than our duty, they seem to notice one's work as if they knew all one's heart had gone out into the brushes, and one's welcome into the polishing and the cleaning."

"Blessed are those servants whom their Lord, when He cometh, shall find waiting," John answers quietly, and half to himself. "Isn't it a bit of a parable, Mary, the getting ready and looking out? Do you mind what our clergyman, down home, said to us when we came away: '*Let in* the love of Christ; *live out* the love *to* Christ; work out the life of Christ; *look on* to the coming of Christ'? If we look out for earthly masters and study to make ready for them, how much more for the One who says, 'Behold, I come quickly!'"

"I want to, John, I want to. It helps me when I see you stand so firm down in the servants' hall, when they laugh at you for your country notions and for 'setting up for a parson,' because you won't play cards and go out to places like the others do. When I see you so steadfast, and answering back friendly, and helping all round, and so happy about your work, doing it all so carefully through and through, I want to be at one with you in it all, John, and I am trying. Oh, John, it's grand to be serving the King, as our teacher used to say, in all the dusting and brushing and sweeping and housework, and to know that doing it with all one's heart is doing it for Him, and getting ready for Him when He comes! But see! there's the carriage!" And Mary is out of sight, while her brother runs down the steps to be in waiting in a moment.

We must not stay. It is well to know that amongst the busy crowd of servants in the gay and busy city there are those who, in their everyday life and in their common duties, are looking and making ready for THE APPEARING, and for the "*Well done, good and faithful servant!*" when the King comes to His own.

Hark! there is a clatter in the streets; a rush, a roar; people are falling back on to the footway; carts hastily backing up side- streets. There, there in the distance you may see the red glare, which tells us what it is all about. The fire-engines are coming along! See the galloping of the horses! Hear the cheering of the crowd!

Oh, how well I remember the sound when I saw our own hospital on fire and when for a few moments there was a lock in the street, until the soldiers came up and cleared the way! There is a minute's pause now at this narrow corner. Here are two of the firemen on the tumbrels; listen to what they are saying as we pass by.

"Hot work to-night, Bill!"

"Looks likely, Tom; we'll be in for it in another five minutes. Grand to be ready, anyway, Tom, living or dying!"

"Aye, '*With you alway*' now, and '*Well done!*' when He comes: that's about worth while having got hold of!" And the way is cleared, and off rush the horses; and

> "Let our hearts be true, brothers,
> To suffer and to do, brothers,"

comes back to our ears as we know that in all the danger and roar, and in the possible death call of the fire, there are some of the "King's own" among the noble band of the fire-brigade, who have a thought in their bravest of all brave callings of the One who ere[1] long will come with a "Well done!" for His own.

But stop where these glittering lights are seen. This is a busy store indeed! In one part sparkling Christmas presents; in another toys to delight the little ones; in another fine dresses, wreaths, flowers, all manner of dazzling finery for the rich and gay. Come upstairs to the thronged workroom, heated with gas, where busy fingers are toiling before the work of the day can be finished. Here

---

[1] Before

are dresses, one after another, of every color and form. Two or three young girls are busy putting the last touches to a robe for some unknown young beauty, who is to dance away Christmas hours in that light gauze with its flowery wreaths.

"It *does* seem hard sometimes that there should be such a difference between the rich and poor," murmurs to her companions one of the three whose heads are bent over the bright folds; "she dancing away in it all, and we up to Christmas Eve working our hearts out to get it done!"

"Would you change, Fanny?" answers gently a quiet girl, with busy touches, working by her side.

"To be sure I would!" returns her companion. "Only give me a chance, and you'll not see me in this stifling workroom another Christmas. A gay life and a merry one for me!"

"Kate don't think so," put in a third speaker, half mockingly. "Kate's a saint; Kate wouldn't go in for a Christmas flare- up; no, not for all the finery in the shop! She's a deal too pious. I wonder what sort of gayeties she'll be up to these holidays! Sunday-school tea and a meeting!—eh, Kate?"

"There might be worse things than that," is the pleasant answer; "but my father's ill, and I shan't be out much. We'll have to keep our Christmas together. The best of my holiday will be it's giving me the chance of staying quiet with him."

"I forgot; I didn't mean to be unkind," answers in a moment the girl who had been mocking a moment before, as she remembers that Kate's father is slowly sinking. "I know it'll be dull for you," she adds, with a little shame for her rude speech.

"*He's not dull*," is the quiet reply; "and he won't let me be downhearted. He said to me when I had to leave him this morning—for we've nothing but what I get here to keep us—he said to me, 'Christmas with "*He loved me and gave Himself for me*" in it is here for you and me, Kitty; and well keep it with Him; and there's a Christmas coming when He'll know us, and say, "I have loved thee with an everlasting love," and will make room for us to be with Him forever, and that's worth everything to look on to.'"

"I suppose there is some truth in all that," says Fanny, with a moment's thought, as she prepares to fasten off the wreath; "but I don't want to think about it. Dear me, if I did! Why, one's life is all the other way. I should go mad if I were to take to thinking of the end, and dying, and dismal things like that!"

"Not dismal things—joy cometh in the morning! that's what it'll be when the Christmas comes which is to bring the King back," whispers Kate, with a thrill in her voice which tells us that she has got something which she wouldn't give up for all the world. "Fanny, dear, shutting your eyes to its coming won't keep off what you don't want to think about, even if it's all trouble. But it's good times on in front: there's real happiness when we've got safe hold for ourselves; and then, even—even in the sorrow, we know that it is all for a little while; and on beyond, think of the King's calling for us and saying, 'I have known thee by name,' and giving us a place with Him in glory!"

The work is finished off; the "hands" are busy in putting away the silks and muslins, and we are back again in the street where Kate's humble home is to be found. But her low voice has seemed, there in the busy workroom, to take up our song:

"Arise, and be of good cheer, brothers;
The day will soon be here, brothers;
The victory is near, brothers;
  When the Lamb shall wear the crown!

There'll be no sad heart in the Morning;
No tear will start in the Morning;
There'll be joy in the Christmas Morning
  When the King comes to His own!

But night is nearing, and it is time we came to an end of our walk. Let us turn up this street. See what a dazzle at the corner! How men—men and women, too!— throng in at the door of that barroom—"THE LION," like a great beast of prey, swinging over their heads! It is a close evening, and some are leaning with their pipes against the wall outside, as a tall workman goes by with a quick step and a blue ribbon in his button-hole.

"That's Jem!" calls out one of the number; "he won't have nothing to do with us now. Saint James he's become since he took up with the Blue Ribboners. He'll be keeping his Christmas going to church with his family, and sit for his picture afterwards in a tract— that's what he'll do!" and a roar of laughter comes from the rest.

"Preach us a sermon, Jem," cried another, barring the way as his old mate passes by.

"Yes, a Christmas sermon, with all our sins for the text," shouts another. "Come along, Jem; I'll be clerk!"

"Fire away, Jem; we'll be congregation and all the rest!" and another shout rings up the street.

"Agreed!" answers, with a sudden turn round, the man who at first had seemed as if he would push by, taking no notice of their taunts. "I'll preach, but mind it's fair all round. If I preach, you come down with a promise to hold hard by my text and think it over after. That's no more than honorable."

"Done, man! We'll hang it up, framed and glazed, for Christmas Eve," chimes in a rough voice from the door of the taproom. "Give it to us, parson!"

"Couldn't do better; it's hung up framed and glazed, so to speak, in my mind," says Blue Ribboner, "and here it is: 'BEHOLD, I COME QUICKLY; *and My reward is with Me, to give every man according as his work shall be.*' There, mates," he adds, "it's the King that's coming that sends that message. He came once to save, and He'll come again to know what you and I have been doing about that salvation that's offered us grand and free, and paid down now, if we'll only take it, and take Him at His word. I've gone in for serving Him, and it's a fine service, I can tell you. There'll be honors and medals then. Privates as well as captains will be remembered when He comes again; and there's not one on that army list that won't know the meaning of 'My reward is with Me.' Good-night to you, and remember *He's coming* as sure as to-morrow's sun will shine."

And as he strikes down the street, a true soldier in a workingman's dress, do you not fancy you hear the song:

We're in for the winning side, brothers,
Bound to the Lord who died, brothers,
We shall see Him glorified, brothers,
    And the Lamb shall wear the crown.

What of the cold world's scorning?
There'll be joy enough in the Morning—
There'll be joy in the Christmas Morning
    When the King comes to His own!"

My reader, we have been our rounds together, and it is time that these Christmas words should end. May I, before we close, put a plain question to you; and it is this, "*What will that Coming be to you*?" For it is all true to-night. Our King is coming, and will be true to His own, and give them a place in His kingdom, because they have gone to Him *now* for pardon, who bore their sins and their punishment on the cross. And His word is given to those who seek Him here, that "Whosoever shall confess Me before men, him shall the Son of man confess before the angels of God." How is it with you? He calls to you now. He wants to save you now. You may be His now. You and I may never meet on earth; but we shall meet then. He will say to each of us one of two words: "DEPART!" or "COME!" Which will it be for you? I entreat you to stop and think, for it will be too late to decide then.

Oh, that together, for His sake who died that now we might lay our sins on a pardoning Sin-bearer, we may share

"The joy of the Christmas Morning
When the King comes to His own!"

ISAIAH 30:21
ROMANS 8:14

PSALM 27:1- GOD'IS asking to do this before the above come there.

Dont worry about Money
God First everything will be in order
You have to Pay a price
Hebrews 6:19 (You go behind the
REVELAT. 2:17

DEUTORONOMY 8:8
GENESIS 26.

Printed in Great Britain
by Amazon

25627400R00037